love to COLOR
ART PUZZLES

A Color By Number Book
of Petals, Patterns, Mandalas and More

Tiffany Lovering

NORTH LIGHT BOOKS
CINCINNATI, OHIO
artistsnetwork.com

Contents

Puzzle 1
page 13

Puzzle 5
page 115

Puzzle 2
page 53

Puzzle 6
page 123

Puzzle 3
page 73

Puzzle 7
page 131

Puzzle 4
page 91

Puzzle 8
page 141

How to Use This Book

Coloring

This book includes eight puzzles of different sizes to color. You can use markers, pencils, crayons or anything that has the number of shades indicated on the palette for each puzzle. Here are some tips for coloring, assembling and displaying these puzzles to make it more fun for you.

Gallery of Color Inspiration

The back of this book has images of the completed colored puzzles along with the palette I used for the images. It is not necessary to use the exact colors I've used. The important thing to remember when coloring each puzzle is to be sure to color by number. For example, if the palette calls for number 1 to be green, but you would rather use orange, make sure to color all number 1's orange. If this isn't done, the continuity of the image onto different pages may be interrupted and make the puzzle more difficult to piece together.

Palettes

Each puzzle has a palette at the bottom to color in. This is to make it easier to keep coloring according to the numbers, especially if you choose your own colors instead of going by the images in the back of the book. The palette will be different for each puzzle, and it is highly recommended to fill in the palette as you color the puzzle pages.

Assembling the Puzzles

Piecing the puzzles together shouldn't be too difficult. Once you figure out where each piece goes, you will need to trim the edges off some of the pages to make them lay perfectly as a large image. Use tape on the back of the pages to keep the puzzle together. Do not use glue, as it will cause the pages to ripple when dry. Tape will also allow you to take the puzzle apart when you no longer wish to display the art.

Displaying the Puzzles

Displaying the puzzles after they are colored and pieced together may require a significant amount of wall space. You may want to consider displaying only a few pages of the puzzle at a time instead of the entire image. The puzzles are designed in a way where you can display as much or as little of the puzzle without it looking awkward so choose your favorite section and display that until you want to change it out with a different section of the same puzzle or a different puzzle.

Share Your Work!

No matter how you choose to color or display the puzzles, the goal of this book is to have fun with it. I hope you will share the finished pieces in the Facebook group: Love to Color and allow others to be inspired by your work.

Puzzle 1 | 20 PIECES

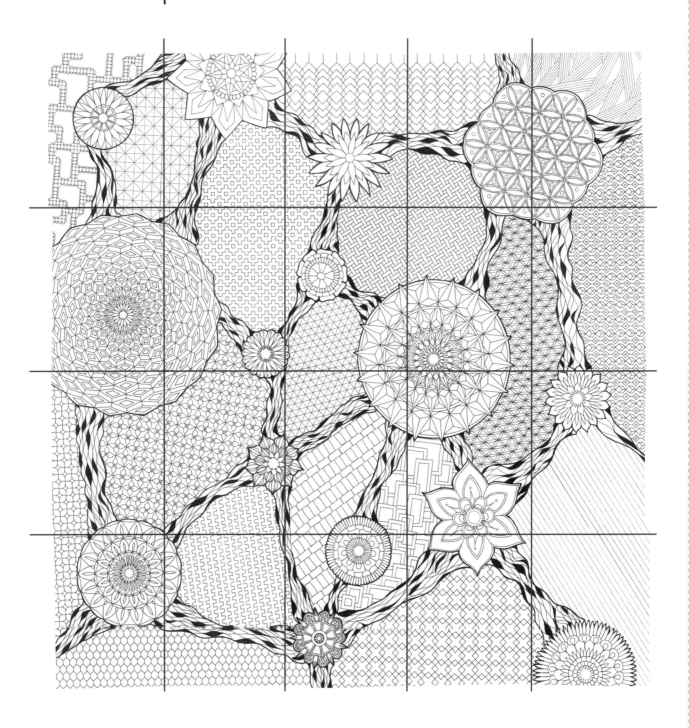

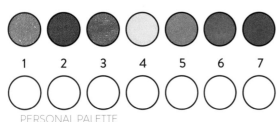

1   2   3   4   5   6   7

PERSONAL PALETTE

Puzzle 2 | 10 PIECES

1 2 3 4 5 6 7 8 9 10 11 12

PERSONAL PALETTE

Puzzle 3 | 9 PIECES

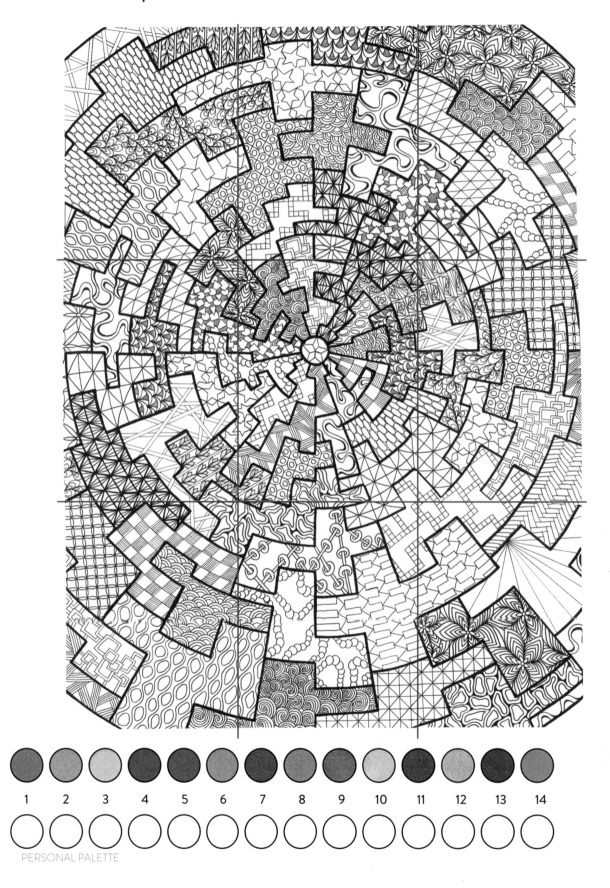

1 2 3 4 5 6 7 8 9 10 11 12 13 14

PERSONAL PALETTE

Puzzle 4 | 12 PIECES

1 2 3 4 5 6 7 8 9 10 11 12 13 14 15 16

PERSONAL PALETTE

Puzzle 5 | 4 PIECES

1 2 3 4 5 6

PERSONAL PALETTE

Puzzle 6 | 4 PIECES

1 2 3 4 5 6 7 8 9 10 11

PERSONAL PALETTE

Puzzle 7 | 5 PIECES

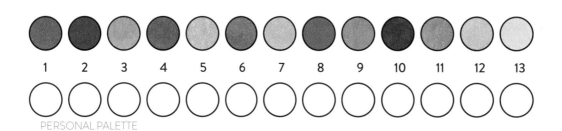

1   2   3   4   5   6   7   8   9   10   11   12   13

PERSONAL PALETTE

Puzzle 8 | 12 PIECES

PERSONAL PALETTE

PUZZLE 1, PIECE 1

PUZZLE 1, PIECE 2

PUZZLE 1, PIECE 3

PUZZLE 1, PIECE 4

PUZZLE 1, PIECE 5

PUZZLE 1, PIECE 6

PUZZLE 1, PIECE 7

PUZZLE 1, PIECE 8

PUZZLE 1, PIECE 9

PUZZLE 1, PIECE 10

PUZZLE 1, PIECE 11

PUZZLE 1, PIECE 12

PUZZLE 1, PIECE 13

PUZZLE 1, PIECE 14

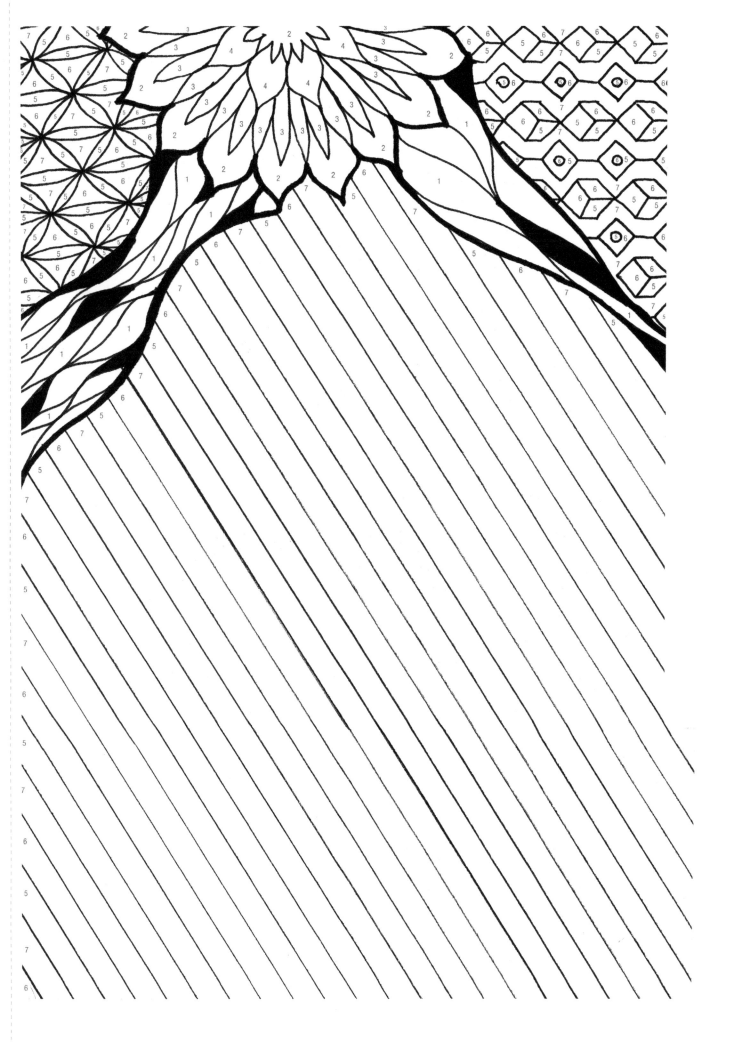

PUZZLE 1, PIECE 15

PUZZLE 1, PIECE 16

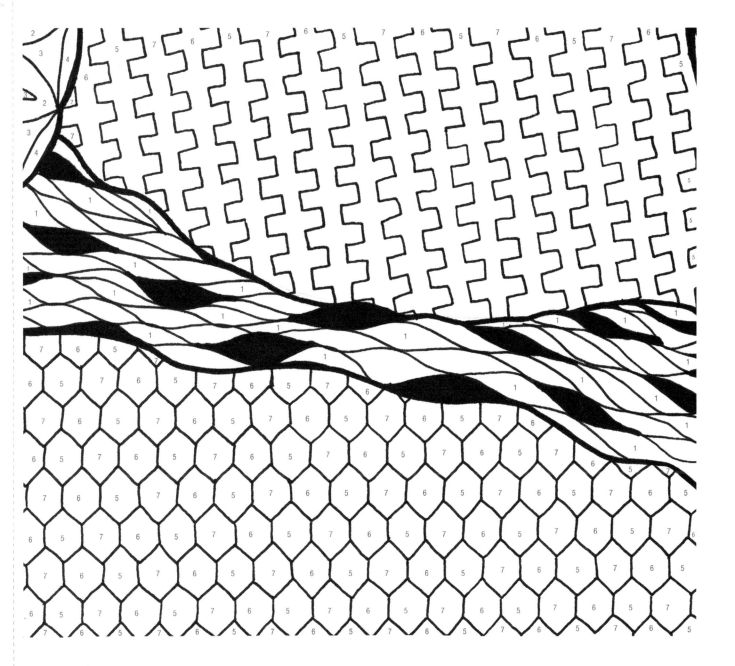

PUZZLE 1, PIECE 17

PUZZLE 1, PIECE 18

PUZZLE 1, PIECE 19

PUZZLE 1, PIECE 20

PUZZLE 2, PIECE 1

PUZZLE 2, PIECE 2

PUZZLE 2, PIECE 3

PUZZLE 2, PIECE 4

PUZZLE 2, PIECE 5

PUZZLE 2, PIECE 6

PUZZLE 2, PIECE 7

PUZZLE 2, PIECE 8

PUZZLE 2, PIECE 9

PUZZLE 2, PIECE 10

PUZZLE 3, PIECE 1

PUZZLE 3, PIECE 2

PUZZLE 3, PIECE 3

PUZZLE 3, PIECE 4

PUZZLE 3, PIECE 5

PUZZLE 3, PIECE 6

PUZZLE 3, PIECE 7

PUZZLE 3, PIECE 8

PUZZLE 3, PIECE 9

PUZZLE 4, PIECE 1

PUZZLE 4, PIECE 2

94

PUZZLE 4, PIECE 3

PUZZLE 4, PIECE 4

PUZZLE 4, PIECE 5

PUZZLE 4, PIECE 6

PUZZLE 4, PIECE 7

PUZZLE 4, PIECE 8

PUZZLE 4, PIECE 9

PUZZLE 4, PIECE 10

PUZZLE 4, PIECE 11

PUZZLE 4, PIECE 12

PUZZLE 5, PIECE 1

PUZZLE 5, PIECE 2

PUZZLE 5, PIECE 3

PUZZLE 5, PIECE 4

PUZZLE 6, PIECE 1

PUZZLE 6, PIECE 2

PUZZLE 6, PIECE 3

PUZZLE 6, PIECE 4

PUZZLE 7, PIECE 1

PUZZLE 7, PIECE 2

PUZZLE 7, PIECE 3

PUZZLE 7, PIECE 4

PUZZLE 7, PIECE 5

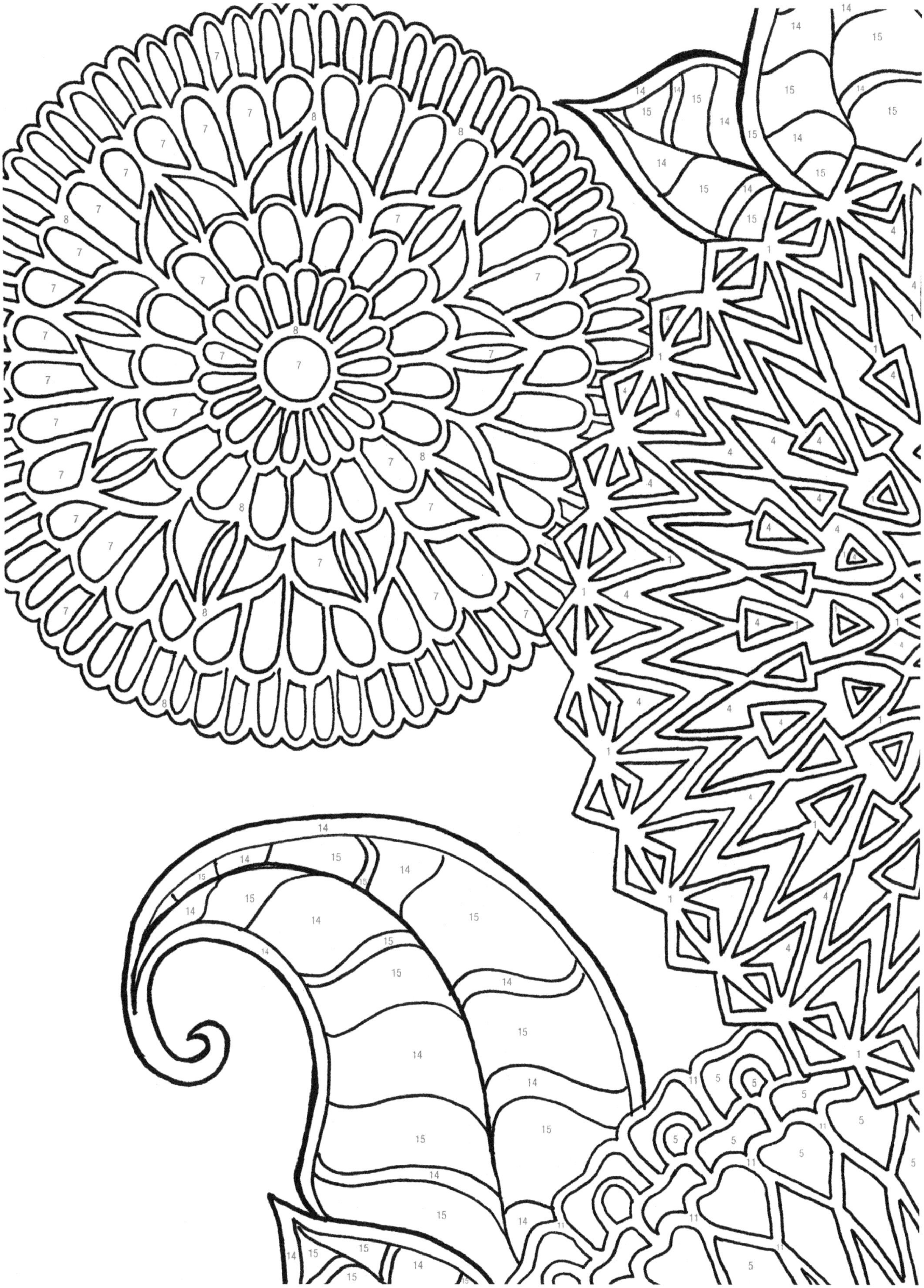

PUZZLE 8, PIECE 1

PUZZLE 8, PIECE 2

PUZZLE 8, PIECE 3

PUZZLE 8, PIECE 4

PUZZLE 8, PIECE 5

PUZZLE 8, PIECE 6

PUZZLE 8, PIECE 7

PUZZLE 8, PIECE 8

PUZZLE 8, PIECE 9

PUZZLE 8, PIECE 10

PUZZLE 8, PIECE 11

PUZZLE 8, PIECE 12

Color Inspiration Gallery

Drawing the designs for these puzzles was a matter of finding patterns that I thought flowed nicely while still having a contrast of soft and hard angles for visual interest. When coloring the patterns within the puzzles, I allowed the world around me to inspire the combination of colors. When I finish drawing a piece, I look at the entire drawing from a slight distance to see what I might not have seen as I was creating it. I think about the different colors I have in my collection and imagine what certain combinations of colors might look like in the drawing. I considered many different possibilities for each puzzle, and I used the color combinations that felt right. While I provided the palette I used for each drawing, if you are inspired to use a different combination of colors, I hope you will go with your own choices.

Puzzle 1

In this puzzle, I wanted the mandalas to be a harsh contrast from the patterns. Taking this into consideration as I stared at the drawing, the mandalas reminded me of asteroids burning through the sky, leaving trails behind. I used oranges, reds and yellows to represent the asteroids and the galaxy colors like blues, purples and greens for the patterns surrounding the mandalas.

Puzzle 2

The coloring of this drawing was inspired by flowers that have close petals such as carnations, roses and chrysanthemums. When petals are close together, if you really look at them, it's not just a red rose. It's a rose with many different shades that are all dependent on the way the light hits the flower. I used that idea in a dramatic way with the colors I chose for this puzzle.

Puzzle 3

The drawing of this puzzle was a remake of a much smaller drawing I did on my YouTube channel in the very early days of my channel. My one regret for that drawing back in 2013 was that I didn't color it. As I looked at this puzzle, it reminded me of a tunnel. I used a lot of contrasting colors within each section to help draw the eye from the outer edges into the center where there's a very simple flower.

Puzzle 4

For this drawing, as well as the next three, I used the four seasons to inspire the coloring. This one has a lot of flowers and swirling vines. It really inspired a feeling of a warm spring breeze, so I used pastel spring colors contrasting with the brighter shades of a summer palette.

Puzzle 5

This zendala made me think of a suncatcher that my mother used to hang as an Easter decoration. I used very pale spring colors that would accentuate the soft lines within the drawing. I used the darker contrast of purple and pink for the center flower to make that the focal point of the drawing.

Puzzle 6

For this drawing, I started thinking of the paisley designs as leaves, and leaves always remind me of the autumn months. I thought of the end of summer where you can smell the scent of autumn in the air and the summer flowers are coming to an end. I used a considerable amount of yellow and orange to add to the feeling of autumn while contrasting the paisley leaves with darker shades of summer flowers.

Puzzle 7

This puzzle really inspired thoughts of the wind and the cold at the end of autumn going into the winter months. The swirling shapes of different contrasting colors were used for the feeling of movement. I used a gray background to represent the sky of winter that always feels heavy, like it might snow at any moment.

Puzzle 8

This puzzle has probably the most obvious inspiration of spring flowers. I colored the mandalas with thoughts of flowers just coming into bloom with vibrant shades. The leaves were colored with different shades of green that young plants and flowers have before fully maturing. I kept the background white as a goodbye to the winter snow when all the green starts coming out into the world again.

Share Your Puzzle Art Online!

The Facebook group, Love to Color, is something I created for coloring enthusiasts to share their coloring art with each other. Join the group today and become inspired by others and share your coloring pieces so others can be inspired by you, too.

I am quite active in this group, leaving comments on artwork and uploading free coloring pages to print that aren't available anywhere else. I hope you will share photos of how you color and display the puzzles in this book.

Puzzle 1

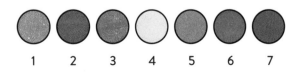

1   2   3   4   5   6   7

Puzzle 2

Puzzle 3

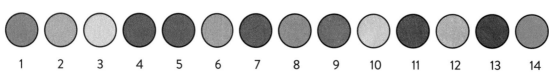

1 2 3 4 5 6 7 8 9 10 11 12 13 14

Puzzle 4

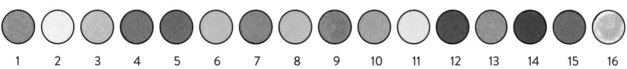

Puzzle 5

1   2   3   4   5   6

Puzzle 6

1 2 3 4 5 6 7 8 9 10 11

Puzzle 7

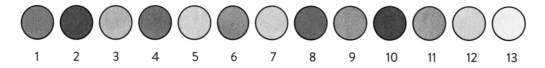

Puzzle 8

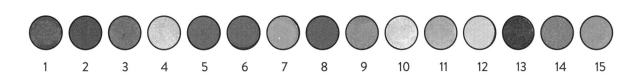

1 2 3 4 5 6 7 8 9 10 11 12 13 14 15

a content + ecommerce company

Other fine North Light Books are available from your favorite bookstore, art supply store or online supplier. Visit our website at fwcommunity.com

21 20 19 18 17   5 4 3 2 1

DISTRIBUTED IN CANADA BY FRASER DIRECT
100 Armstrong Avenue
Georgetown, ON, Canada L7G 5S4
Tel: (905) 877-4411

DISTRIBUTED IN THE U.K. AND EUROPE
BY F&W MEDIA INTERNATIONAL LTD
Pynes Hill Court, Pynes Hill, Rydon Lane, Exeter,
EX2 5AZ, UK
Tel: (+44) 1392 797680
Email: enquiries@fwmedia.com

ISBN 13: 978-1-4403-5052-8

Edited by Sarah Laichas and Beth Erikson
Designed by Geoff Raker
Production coordinated by Jennifer Bass

About the Author

Tiffany Lovering started tangling as a fun and relaxing craft in between writing novels. As she learned the art of creating different patterns and techniques, tangling quickly became a passion she wanted to share with others.

In 2013 she created a YouTube channel dedicated to showing others her tangling techniques. She has since amassed more than 500 videos, 65,000 subscribers and 7 million views (and going strong!). In addition to YouTube, she has created a small Facebook community where fans can participate in a monthly tangle swap. She writes a blog discussing her inspiration and the processes of her more popular tangles.

Tiffany has produced three North Light DVDs that cover tangle tips, techniques and patterns. She also teaches several online courses on tangling and mandalas throughout the year.

In addition to the art of tangling, Tiffany is passionate about reading and has a book review blog. She currently has four novels and one short story available on Amazon. She resides in Tennessee with her daughter, Allison.

Connect with Tiffany!

You Tube youtube.com/tiffanylovering

BLOG: tiffanytangles.blogspot.com

 facebook.com/TiffanyTangles

 twitter.com/tiffanylovering

Dedication

This book is dedicated to the best big brother in the whole world, Greg Lovering. Thank you for making me laugh, encouraging me when I need it and sharing my accomplishments whenever you can. I love you!

Ideas. Instruction. Inspiration.

Receive FREE downloadable bonus materials when you sign up for our free newsletter at artistsnetwork.com/newsletter_thanks.

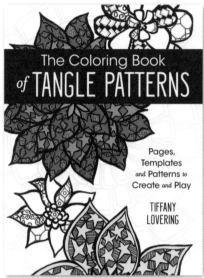

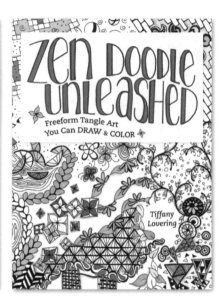

Get your art in print!

Visit artistsnetwork.com/competitions for up-to-date information on North Light art competitions.